Genre Expository Text

Essential Question

How do people meet environmental challenges?

AGROUND!

THE STORY OF THE *EXXON VALDEZ*

BY SANDY McKAY

I0800881

Introduction 2

Chapter 1
The Spill 4

Chapter 2
The Cleanup 8

Chapter 3
The Effects 11

Conclusion 16

Respond to Reading 18

PAIRED READ **Speaking Her Mind** 19

Glossary 22

Index 23

STEM **Focus on Science** 24

INTRODUCTION

Imagine not having DVDs, telephones, or even your sneakers. Many things we use every day are made from oil. Oil is found in rocks in Earth's crust, or outer layer. Oil in rocks is called crude oil.

Edwin Drake drilled the first oil well in the United States in 1859.

Thousands of years ago, people found small amounts of crude oil **seeping** from the ground. They used it as fuel for lamps. They also used it to make paints and medicines.

Then in 1859, people drilled into Earth to make America's first oil well. Oil wells **extract** oil from the ground. Next, people looked for ways to **refine**, or take the dirt out of, the oil. Cleaning the oil allowed them to use it in new ways.

They boiled the oil to separate it into different parts called fractions. One of these fractions is the gasoline that we use in cars.

These days, we use refined oil in many ways. We use it to make plastics, paints, and **synthetic** cloth such as polyester.

Many businesses around the world use oil. That oil has to be carried to them. The easiest way to **transport** large amounts of oil is on ships called oil tankers. However, using tankers can be risky. Tankers can crash into other tankers. They can also run into rocks or sand under the water.

OIL TANKER—SIDE VIEW

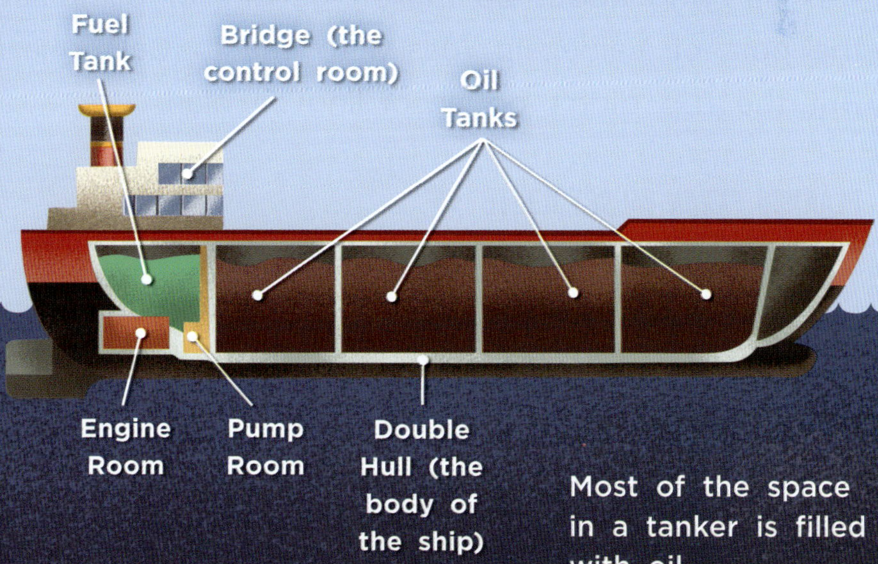

Most of the space in a tanker is filled with oil.

CHAPTER 1

THE SPILL

The *Exxon Valdez* was about 987 feet long and 166 feet wide. It carried up to 62 million gallons of oil.

The *Exxon Valdez* was a huge ship called a supertanker. Supertankers transport millions of gallons of oil around the world.

On Thursday, March 23, 1989, the *Exxon Valdez* was carrying about 53 million gallons of oil. It left the port of Valdez in Alaska to sail to California. But the trip didn't go according to plan.

PLANNED *EXXON VALDEZ* ROUTE TO CALIFORNIA

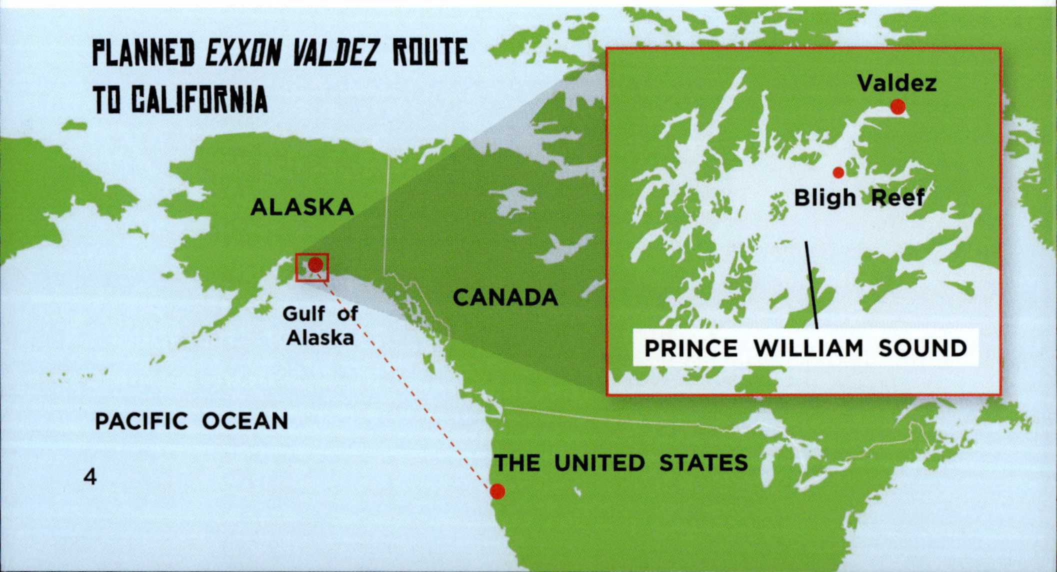

Two hours after leaving, the crew changed course to avoid hitting icebergs. The crew didn't know that they had steered the tanker straight for Bligh Reef. This reef is a huge underwater rock wall in Prince William Sound.

The tanker hit the reef just after midnight on Friday, March 24. Sharp boulders **punctured**, or poked holes in, the side of the tanker. Oil immediately began leaking into the sea.

The crew tried to move the tanker off the reef. It was stuck. The **collision** had punctured eight tanks full of oil. Seven million gallons of oil oozed into the ocean in four hours. There were still millions of gallons of oil on the ship.

OIL AND WATER

Oil and water do not mix. Crude oil floats on top of the ocean. It floats because it is lighter than seawater. A large amount of oil on the surface of the ocean is called a **slick**.

Sunlight or bacteria can break down oil slicks. But oil breaks down slowly in cold water.

The tanker's captain called the **Coast Guard** for help. The Coast Guard made emergency phone calls to the tanker's owners and to experts around the world.

These people had to think quickly. They had never experienced such a large oil spill. First, a tugboat sailed out to the tanker to rescue the crew. Next, the port of Valdez was closed so that no other ships could come in.

The response team at the port needed special equipment as quickly as possible. They had to stop the spill and get the oil out of the water. But the equipment they needed was very far away. The spilled oil was spreading fast.

Other tankers had to wait out at sea while the port of Valdez was closed.

It was hard for the response team to find the special equipment that they needed. Early Sunday morning, the team was still loading equipment onto boats. They worked as fast as they could.

Experts and volunteers from all over the world came to help.

STOP AND CHECK

What happened to the *Exxon Valdez*?

RESPONSE TIME

"Rapid response is important. As the oil spreads out, it becomes more **viscous** and hard to **disperse** ... An oil spill is like a house burning down. You've got to be ready. You can't just stand around trying to figure it out ... If you wait, you might as well not bother at all."

—Dr. James Butler, National Academy of Sciences

CHAPTER 2

THE CLEANUP

By Sunday afternoon, the oil slick had spread farther. Even worse, a storm was coming.

Some equipment for cleaning up the oil couldn't be used in storms. Also, a storm could move the slick closer to land. If the oil reached the shore, it would badly damage the beaches and harm the animals.

The response team tried different ways to remove the spilled oil. First, they tried to burn the oil. They placed a **boom**, or floating barrier, around the spill. Then they set fire to the oil trapped inside. Unfortunately, a lot of oil was already outside the boom.

Burning oil at sea is usually the fastest way to get rid of a slick.

The team also used skimmers to scoop up the oil inside the boom. This was a slow method, and the weather had become a terrible **inconvenience**. The storm stirred up the water, which caused the oil to mix with seaweed. The oily seaweed clogged the skimmers.

By Sunday night, the skimmers had scooped up only 12,500 gallons of oil. More than 10 million gallons had been spilled. The slick now covered 100 square miles (161 square kilometers).

On Monday, airplanes sprayed chemicals over the slick. They were trying to dissolve, or break up, the oil. But this method didn't work. After that, it was too late. The oil reached the shore.

The chemicals sprayed into the ocean didn't mix well with the oil.

U.S. Coast Guard photo by Petty Officer 3rd Class Stephen Lehmann

CLEANUP METHODS

Many methods were used to clean up the *Exxon Valdez* oil spill.

Absorbents: used to soak up oil like a sponge

Boom: a floating barrier put around an oil slick to keep it from spreading

Burning: good for cleaning up a spill but makes a lot of smoke

Dispersants: break up oil into tiny droplets and force it to sink

Fertilizer: causes oil-eating bacteria to eat the oil more quickly

Pumping: sucking up the skimmed oil into a storage tank

Skimming: scooping oil from the surface of the water

STOP AND CHECK

How well did the cleanup methods work?

THE EFFECTS

Thick, gooey oil soon covered the beaches. The storm flung oil up into trees. The area became a disaster zone.

About 11 million gallons of oil spilled from the *Exxon Valdez*. That much oil would fill 17 Olympic-size swimming pools.

Within a week, there were dead animals all over the beaches. Many volunteers came in a hurry to help animals that were sick.

The oil was **poisonous** to animals. That is why they got so sick. Oil also stuck to animals' fur or feathers. The fur or feathers **matted** together and couldn't keep the animals warm.

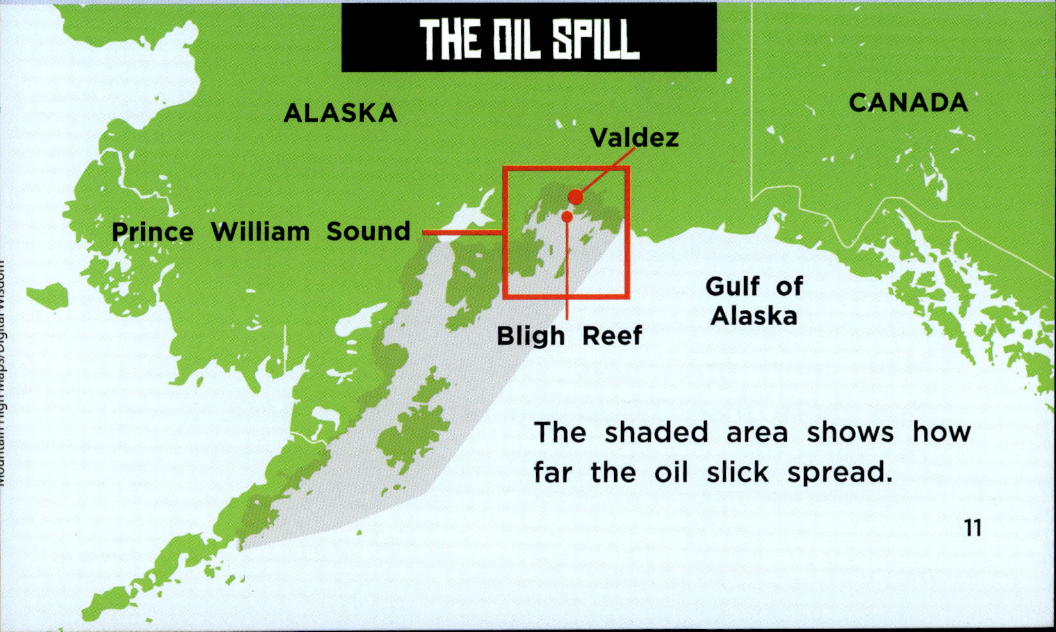

The shaded area shows how far the oil slick spread.

Many animals froze to death because their fur or feathers were covered with oil. Others died from starvation or from swallowing the oil.

About 10,000 volunteers helped with the cleanup.

The volunteers tried hard to save the animals. They washed birds with warm, soapy water and used toothbrushes to gently scrub their feathers. Then they rinsed off the soap and oil.

The oil also hurt or killed a lot of sea otters. Some otters went blind when the oil got in their eyes.

The volunteers washed the otters in soapy water. They gave them food through tubes. It sometimes took several hours to clean one otter.

THE TOLL

The hard work of volunteers saved many birds, but many other birds didn't survive. About 250,000 seabirds died because of the oil spill.

Rescuers also found about 1,000 dead otters. Many more must have died at sea. Experts think that more than 3,000 sea otters died because of the oil spill.

THE HUMAN IMPACT

The *Exxon Valdez* oil spill had a **prolonged** effect on Prince William Sound. Before the spill, fishing **generated** many jobs for local people. Afterward, fishers could not sell the fish they caught. It was not safe for people to eat.

STOP AND CHECK

How were animals affected by the oil spill?

Fred McConnaughey/Science Source

Salmon farms like this could not avoid the spreading oil.

The community of Prince William Sound changed, too. Many people lost their jobs and had to move away.

The local people were angry. They thought that the oil companies had caused an **eclipse** of their community's power. The people wanted to be included in what happened next.

As a result, the people formed a **watchdog group**. This group **monitors**, or watches, how the tankers affect the environment.

The watchdog group makes sure that oil tankers work safely.

The *Exxon Valdez* oil spill had a horrible effect on Prince William Sound. It damaged more than 1,300 miles (2,100 kilometers) of coastline. Thousands of fish, seabirds, and otters died, even though the volunteers' **tenacity** saved many creatures.

Scientists still argue about how well the area has recovered. Some say the area has returned to normal. Others say that some animals are not breeding as much as before. **Periodic** monitoring of these species will continue for many years.

STOP AND CHECK

How did the oil spill affect local people and the environment?

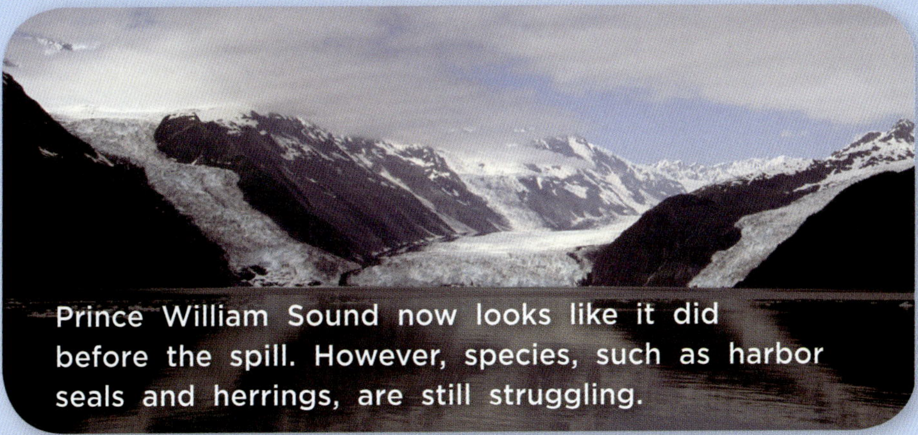

Prince William Sound now looks like it did before the spill. However, species, such as harbor seals and herrings, are still struggling.

CONCLUSION

The *Exxon Valdez* oil spill was a **calamity**. It has taken decades for Prince William Sound to recover. Some scientists say it still isn't back to the way it was before the spill.

Many people learned from the spill. People who transport oil build supertankers to be stronger now. The Coast Guard uses a satellite to watch tankers travel through the sound. Trained sea pilots get on tankers at Bligh Reef and steer the ships past the reef.

Cleanup equipment has also been improved. Skimmers can now scoop up much more oil. Forty miles (64 kilometers) of boom are stored in Prince William Sound.

It took 14 hours for a boom to reach the *Exxon Valdez* oil spill.

There is also more **awareness** of what can go wrong when transporting oil. People understand the dangers. The Coast Guard has oil spill drills, just like school fire drills. People involved in transporting oil know that everyone needs to be organized and work together. By being in **alignment**, they can reduce the risks.

These risks can have tragic effects. The people of Prince William Sound know this firsthand. They are determined to keep another accident from happening.

Many people still visit Prince William Sound to see this wilderness area.

Palladium/Age Fotostock

Respond to Reading

Summarize

Use key details from *Aground!* to summarize the selection. Your graphic organizer may help you.

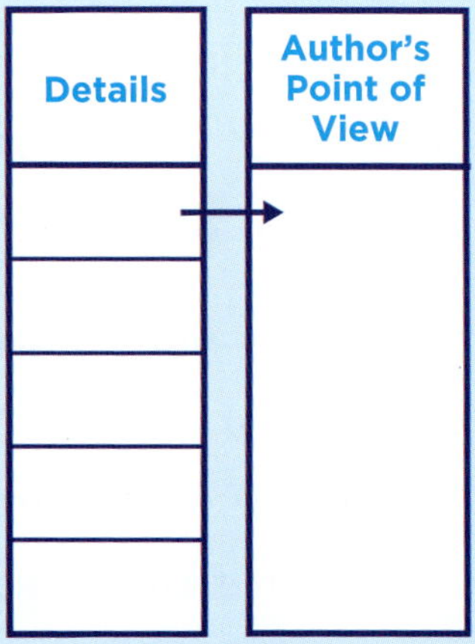

Text Evidence

1. What is the author's point of view toward the volunteers in Chapter 3? Describe two details that show this. **AUTHOR'S POINT OF VIEW**

2. Find the word *dissolve* on page 9. What clues help you to understand the word's meaning? **VOCABULARY**

3. Reread the conclusion. Does the author think we are better prepared for oil spills now? Write about the author's point of view. **WRITE ABOUT READING**

Genre Biographical Sketch

Compare Texts

Read a speech that asked world leaders to meet environmental challenges.

Speaking Her Mind

Severn Cullis-Suzuki was 12 years old when she made a speech to the **United Nations**.

Severn felt strongly about protecting the environment. She helped form the Environmental Children's Organization (ECO). This group taught children about environmental problems. But Severn also wanted adults to know how children felt.

As a result, Severn and her friends from ECO decided to go to the 1992 United Nations **Earth Summit** in Brazil.

Severn asked the people at the summit to stop damaging the planet. Here is an excerpt from her speech.

Severn Cullis-Suzuki spoke at the United Nations Earth Summit.

Severn Cullis-Suzuki

Address to the Plenary Session, Earth Summit, Rio Centro, Brazil, 1992

Hello, I'm Severn Suzuki speaking for ECO—the Environmental Children's Organization. We are a group of 12- and 13-year-olds trying to make a difference.

Coming up here today, I have no hidden agenda. I am fighting for my future. I am here to speak for all generations to come. I am here to speak on behalf of the starving children around the world whose cries go unheard. I am here to speak for the countless animals dying across this planet because they have nowhere left to go.

I'm only a child, and I don't have all the solutions. I want you to realize neither do you! You don't know how to fix the holes in our ozone layer. You don't know how to bring the salmon back up a dead stream.

At school, even in kindergarten, you teach us to behave in the world. You teach us:

- to clean up our mess
- not to hurt other creatures
- to share—not be greedy.

Then why do you go out and do the things you tell us not to do? ... You grownups say you love us, but I challenge you, please, make your actions reflect your words.

Thank you.

Make Connections

What did Severn ask people to do about environmental challenges? **ESSENTIAL QUESTION**

What connections can you make between Severn's speech and the *Exxon Valdez* disaster? **TEXT TO TEXT**

Glossary

boom *(bewm)* temporary floating barriers ***(page 8)***

Coast Guard *(kohst gahrd)* a branch of the United States armed forces that protects the nation's coastline ***(page 6)***

collision *(kuh-LI-zhuhn)* the act of hitting or running into something ***(page 5)***

disperse *(di-SPUHRS)* to make something break up or spread widely ***(page 7)***

Earth Summit *(urth SUM-it)* a special meeting of the United Nations countries to discuss environmental issues ***(page 19)***

extract *(ek-STRAKT)* to pull out ***(page 2)***

matted *(MAT-id)* clumped or tangled ***(page 11)***

seeping *(SEEP-ing)* oozing or flowing slowly through something ***(page 2)***

slick *(slik)* a layer of oil floating on water ***(page 5)***

synthetic *(sin-THET-ik)* made with chemicals rather than substances found in nature ***(page 3)***

United Nations *(yoo-NIGH-tid NAY-shuhns)* an organization of countries that works to encourage peace, security, and cooperation ***(page 19)***

viscous *(VIS-kuhs)* thick and sticky ***(page 7)***

watchdog group *(WAHCH-dawg grewp)* a group that keeps a close watch on a problem ***(page 14)***

Index

Alaska, *4, 11*

Cullis-Suzuki, Severn, *19–21*

Exxon Valdez oil spill,

- environmental impact, *15*
- human impact, *13–14*
- lessons learned, *16–17*

oil spill cleanup methods, *8–10*

Prince William Sound, *5, 11, 13–17*

Focus on Science

Purpose To understand the properties of oil and water

Procedure

You will need a screw-top jar, water, and some cooking oil. You will also need a feather and a few drops of dish-washing liquid.

Step 1 Half-fill the jar with water. Add 2 teaspoons of oil. Watch how the oil floats on the water.

Step 2 Screw the lid on the jar. Now shake the jar up and down ten times. Put the jar down and watch what happens to the oil.

Step 3 Take the lid off the jar. Dip the feather into the oil and water. Then take it out. Watch what happens to the feather.

Step 4 Now add a few drops of dishwashing liquid to the jar. Screw on the lid. Shake the jar up and down ten times. Watch what happens.

Conclusion What did you see after each of the steps? What have you learned about oil spills in the ocean?